WASPs

OF

WWII

BEN R. GAMES, PhD

D1248614

Fideli
Publishing

ISBN: 978-1-60414-162-7

Editing by Robin Surface

Author's Statement
FACTS
Prologue
Story
Pictures

WASPs

WWII

www.FideliPublishing.com

Pictures from Historical Documents & the Journal of Ben R. Games, PhD

STATEMENT

This is an autobiographical story about one of the author's flying misadventures while serving as a US Army Air Force's acceptance check pilot for the Women Army Service Pilot (WASP) training program in 1944. Lucky for the author that Avenger Field, Sweetwater, Texas, was an

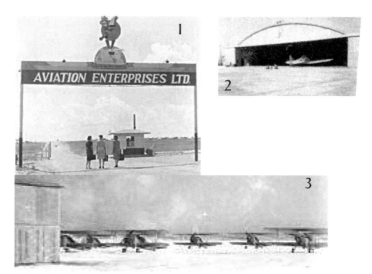

Photo 1, The front gate at Avenger Field, May 1944. Aviation Enterprises Limited, a civilian contractor, ran the field. Photo 2, instrument training area, 1944. Photo 3, planes lined up on the field, courtesy of The Woman's Collection, Texas Woman's University. Used with permission.

open field with no runways or control tower, with a Tetrahedron in the center to indicate the direction of landing. Lucky, because he used the entire field and only missed the Tetrahedron because it was in the center as he bounced a BT-13 on all four sides around it during one landing.

History may have recorded that it was President Truman and the atomic bomb that ended WWII, but the author isn't sure. He has always thought that maybe Jacqueline Cochran may have notified the Japanese Air Force to watch out for him because he was on the way.

Flight line and tower, Avenger Field

Headquarters, Avenger Field.

Avenger Field from the air.

PERSONAL HISTORY FACTS

During WW-1I women started to expand their family duties to help America's war efforts. Nearly 600,000 women joined the military services, while others worked in factories building the planes that their husbands, brothers, and sons flew to fight the enemy. Over 1,000 women pilots attended the US Army women pilot training school at Avenger Field, Texas, to become WASPs (Women Army Service Pilots). All private sports flying was canceled by the government during the war years, yet if men were going to fly then nothing would stop women from joining them. **That's a FACT.**

Helen M. Amsden (18) ran-away to Texas and became the wife of the author on 5 June 1943. They were married in Fort Stockton, Texas, where he was learning to fly the Fairchild PT-19 at Gibbs Field. There were no private planes available, so she attended Army Pilots Ground School and later the USAF jet instrument school. In January 1944 she started flying the Army BT-13, C-45, & B-25. Time changed and in 1946 she flew a L-5 in Japan. During the Korean War in 1950 on Okinawa, she flew with her husband on a combat patrol mission as the Radar Operator in

5

his F-82H. As times changed again, she became Whirly Girl #86 on 20 February 1965, and flew combat in an OH-6 and UH-1 at Bearcat Vietnam. **That's a FACT.** (Ref: *The Terrorist Mirror* and *The Bangkok Drop*)

During the last 67 years Helen Games has raised two sons and established homes in France, Japan, Okinawa, Grand Turk, BWI, and Vietnam. She also continued her education and obtained a MBA in Business. Both of her sons served in Vietnam Ben Jr. (25) with the US Navy in DaNang and Jon R. (16) Army and flew as a helicopter pilot at Bearcat. The author has written that many times when they are speaking as a husband and wife about a mission or even about a single flight, Helen will tell him that she could have done it better. Ben is not quick to agree, but will admit that sometimes she could have. As a wife, Helen has never asked, "What was the body count?" In fact they have never notched a gun, painted a picture of a bomb, or made any marks on their aircraft to indicate a score. Helen is also a FAA licensed sailplane and glider pilot. **That's a FACT.** (Ref: *Balls of Fire*)

There used to be light lines from the east coast to the west coast and through the mountain passes. Helen and Ben often flew together, but not always in the same plane. One evening they stopped at the lake front airport in Cleveland, Ohio, for a night on the town. As they landed, a wind gust blew the prop wash of Ben's LA-4 Lake so Helen flew into it with her LA-4. It was an exciting few minutes as her plane danced around. After they parked, Helen was giving Ben a tongue lashing saying it was all his fault and he wasn't even in her plane. When the FAA Safety inspector drove up all he saw was two new LA-4 planes parked side by side and a wife giving her husband hell. He must've been married, because all he did was get back in his car and leave. The next morning when Ben radioed the control tower for take-off for a flight of two, the controller radioed and asked if the other pilot was his wife. Upon receiving an affirmative answer, he radioed, "Cleared when *she's* ready." **That's a FACT.** (Ref: *My Guardian Angel*)

Helen is a good formation pilot. It doesn't matter if she is leading or flying the wing position or even if it is in a sailplane. One winter day she was flying a Piper Tri-pacer with her two sons as passengers, and Ben was flying the wing slot in a single place Knight Twister. They left the National Guard Base at Fort Wayne, Indiana, on their way to Mid-way Field. Ben had no radios

Ben and Helen Games and their children standing with one of the planes Ben flew "by sight" in World War II.

or flight instruments so he flew very close to Helen's right side. When she made her landing approach, the snow had frozen the Tri-pacer's nose gear in a 30° position. She knew what was going to happen and it did, but Ben had to use her plane as a reference to continue flying. The snowplows had piled the snow up in rows three feet high, and the cross wind was twenty miles per hour with blowing snow. She kept the plane's nose up until the ground speed was about ten miles per hour. When the plane hit the runway it turned into a snow bank stopping with the tail straight up. Ben made a 360° turn around the Tri-pacer as all he could see was the wing and tail

Helen "Whirly Girl" Games was the 86th woman to fly a helicopter. She flew an OH-6 and a UH-1 in combat at Bearcat Vietnam.

lights of the Tri-pacer acting as a lighted pylon. When he was headed directly into the wind, he shut off the engine with the Magneto Switch and turned the prop with the starter so it was parallel with the wings. When the plane hit the snow, it went up on its nose so there were now two pylons marking the snow bank. All Ben had to do was to climb out, help Helen get the children out so they could pull the tails down, and brush the snow out of the air intakes. By the time the crash crews got to them, Helen was shaking the oldest boy and had spanked the youngest son. They wanted their mother to do it again! **That's a FACT.**

Jackie Cochran, considered to be one of the most gifted racing pilots of her generation, in the cockpit of the Canadair Sabre with Chuck Yeager.

WASP FACTS

In September 1940, with the war raging throughout Europe, female aviator Jackie Cochran wrote to Eleanor Roosevelt and proposed starting a women's flying division in the Army Air Forces. She felt that qualified women pilots could do all of the domestic, non-combat aviation jobs required during the war effort, releasing more male pilots for combat. **That's a FACT.**

That same year, Cochran also wrote another letter to Lt. Col. Robert Olds, who was helping to organize the Air Corps Ferrying Command for the Air Corps at the time. (Ferrying Command was originally a courier/aircraft delivery service, but evolved into the air transport branch of the United States Army Air Forces as the Air Transport Command.) In the letter, Cochran suggested that women pilots be employed to fly non-combat missions for the new command. **That's a FACT.**

In early 1941, Colonel Olds asked Cochran to find out how many women pilots there were in the United States, what their flying times and skills were, as well as their interest in flying for the country. She used records from the Civil Aeronautics Administration to gather this data. **That's a FACT.**

In spite of pilot shortages, Lieutenant General Henry H. "Hap" Arnold was the person who needed to be convinced that women pilots were the solution to his staffing problems. Arnold, Chief of the Air Corps, continued as commanding general of the Army Air Forces upon its creation in June 1941. He knew that women were being used successfully in the Air Transport Auxiliary (ATA) in England, so in June 1941 he suggested that Cochran take a group of qualified female pilots to see how the British operation worked. He promised her that no decisions regarding women flying for the USAAF would be made until she returned. **That's a FACT.**

Cochran asked 76 of the most qualified female pilots — identified during the research she had done earlier for Colonel Robert Olds — to come along and fly for the ATA. Qualifications for these women were high, including at least 300 hours of flying time, but most of the women pilots had more than 1,000 hours. They were interviewed and went to Montreal for a physical exam and flight check. The washout rate was high, and only 25 women passed the tests. Two months later, in March 1942, they went to Britain with Cochran to join the ATA. **That's a FACT.**

In September of 1942, while Cochran was in England, General Arnold authorized the formation of the Women's Auxiliary Ferrying Squadron (WAFS) under the direction of Nancy Harkness Love. The WAFS began at Castle Air Base in Wilmington, Delaware with a handpicked group of female pilots whose objective was to ferry military aircraft. Cochran immediately returned from England when she learned of the formation of the WAFS. **That's a FACT.**

PT-17

PT-13 Kaydet

Her experience in Britain had convinced her that women pilots could be trained to do much more than ferrying. She persuaded General Arnold that women were capable of expanded flying duties, and he sanctioned the creation of the Women's Flying Training Detachment (WFTD nicknamed the "Woofteddies") with Cochran heading up the operation. **That's a FACT.**

In August 1943, the WAFS and the WFTD merged to create the Women Airforce Service Pilots (WASP) with Cochran as director and Nancy Love as head of the ferrying division. As director of the WASPs, Cochran supervised the training of hundreds of women pilots at the Avenger Field in Sweetwater, Texas. For her war

BT-13

efforts, she received the Distinguished Service Medal and the Distinguished Flying Cross. *(Source: Wikipedia.)* **That's a FACT.**

Both the PT-13 and PT-17 were named the Kaydet. One of the differences between the two was that the PT-17 had the rear cockpit fitted

AT-6 Texan

Jacqueline Cochran and Gen. Hap Arnold.

Jacqueline Cochran, center, with trainees.

for a cover so that students could get used to flying basic instruments. There was no intercom or radio, and the instructor had to use a gosport tube to give instructions to the student. **That's a FACT.**

WASP students had to be accepted by Army Check Pilots before being hired as Service Pilots for the US Army Air Forces. The final acceptance ride was in a BT-13 Basic Trainer. **That's a FACT.**

Advance training for all single engine schools was in the North American Aviation AT-6 Texan. Each advance training school also had Link Trainers and the students were given ten (10) hours Link time before graduation. **That's a FACT.**

General Hap Arnold and Jacqueline Cochran used an Army B-25 to fly from Bolling Field

*Some of the women pilots standing at the sign
marking the area where no men were allowed, left.
Lt. Crew and Lt. Games standing behind the same sign
after the women moved out.*

in Washington, D.C., to Avenger Field in Sweetwater, Texas in October of 1944 to notify the women pilots that theirs would be the last class to graduate. They met in the gym with the students at 1900 hours. The primary contract flight schools for Aviation Cadets were also closed. **That's a FACT.**

After returning to Goodfellow Field, Lt. Ben R. Games received an Army Commendation Letter for a job well done. Mrs. Jacqueline Cochran did not sign the letter. **That's a FACT.**

1941 - 1943

1943 - 1947

An interesting unrecorded fact was that Lieutenant Crew, Ben's roommate during this assignment, slept in the nude or bare-ass naked due to the heat in Texas and no air-conditioning system. Ben slept in boxer under-shorts and kept his uniform on a chair next to his cot. **That's a FACT.**

At midnight on the day of the General's visit, the women formed a corridor from the check pilots' room toward the gate. They were all armed and ready with pillows, and knocked on the door until Lt. Games answered. He was dressed in his pants, but no shoes or shirt. **That's a FACT.**

The girls pushed past Ben and into the room swinging their pillows. Lt. Crew tried to grab his pillow to cover himself, but he ended up with just the pillowcase. He was calling for help, but Ben remembered that Lt. Crew had just laughed when *he* was in trouble on the flight line. So, Ben started laughing, held the door open and told him to run for the gate entrance guardhouse. Even barefooted, Lt. Crew could sure run! **That's a FACT.**

The next day a WASP student who needed a cross-country flight before graduation was assigned to fly Lt. Games home to San Angelo, Texas. After he signed her Form 5 stating that she was cleared for cross-country flight, she returned to Avenger Field. **That's a FACT.**

The rule of not speaking to any Army Check Pilots had been enforced the entire time the women were at Avenger Air Field. Even though the rule was no longer in affect, Ben's pilot flew the whole flight to Goodfellow Air Base without ever speaking a word. **That's a FACT.**

The Women's Army Auxiliary Corps organized in 1942 and became a part of the US Army in 1943. Later it was renamed the Women's Army Corps (WACs). **That's a FACT.**

The WACs got a better reputation in the Army Air Forces (AAF) than in other branches. Nearly half of the women in the Army were "Air WACs." About half of the Air WACs were in administrative jobs, but they served in 200 different specialties, and 600 of them were in aircraft maintenance. The number of Air WACs peaked at 38,282 in 1944. Women also served as military nurses, including 500 who were AAF flight nurses. **That's a FACT.**

Unlike the Air WACs the WASPs never became full-fledged members of the AAF. **That's a FACT.**

WASPs wore uniforms, but their actual status was civil service. General Hap Arnold was a strong supporter. More than 1,500 WASP pilots served with the AAF, ferrying airplanes from point to point, flying instrument weather, administration, cargo, and towing targets. They flew 77 different kinds of aircraft, from P-38 fighters to B-17 bombers. In 1977, former WASPs were awarded military veteran status with limited benefits. **That's a FACT.**

All records of the WASPs were classified and sealed for 35 years, so their contributions to the war effort were little known and inaccessible to historians for many years. In 1975, under the leadership of Col. Bruce Arnold, son of General Hap Arnold, the WASPs fought the "Battle of Congress" in Washington, D.C., to belatedly obtain recognition as veterans of WWII. **That's a FACT.**

**WWII Victory
Medal**   **American Campaign
Medal**

They organized as a group again and tried to gain public support for their official recognition. Finally, in 1977, with the important support of Senator Barry Goldwater, President Jimmy Carter signed legislation #95-202, Section 401 — the G.I. Bill Improvement Act of 1977 — granting the WASP corps the distinction of full military status for their service. **That's a FACT.**

In 1984, each WASP was awarded the WWII Victory Medal. Those who served for more than one year were also awarded American Theater Ribbon/American Campaign Medals for their service during WWII. Many women died before this came about, and the medals were given to their sons and daughters. **That's a FACT.**

On July 1, 2009, President Barack Obama and the United States Congress awarded the members of the WASP the Congressional Gold Medal. Three of the roughly 300 surviving WASPs were on hand to witness the event. During the ceremony President Obama said, "The Women Airforce Service Pilots courageously answered

President Barack Obama signs S.614 in the Oval Office July 1 at the White House. The bill awards a Congressional Gold Medal to Women Airforce Service Pilots. The WASP program was established during World War II, and from 1942 to 1943, more than 1,000 women joined, flying 60 million miles of noncombat military missions. Of the women who received their wings as Women Airforce Service Pilots, approximately 300 are living today. The women in this photo are Rep. Ileana Ros-Lehtinen, Women's Airforce Service Pilots Elaine Danforth Harmon, Lorraine Z. Rodgers and Bernice Falk Haydu, and active duty USAF pilots Colonel Dawn Dunlop, Colonel Bobbi Doorenbos, Lieutenant Colonel Wendy Wasik, Major Kara Sandifur and Major Nicole Malachowski (former Thunderbird pilot).

their country's call in a time of need while blazing a trail for the brave women who have given and continue to give so much in service to this nation since. Every American should be grateful for their service, and I am honored to sign this bill to finally give them some of the hard-earned recognition they deserve." **That's a FACT.**

On March 10, 2010, 200 surviving WASPs came to the US Capitol to accept the Congressional Gold Medal from House Speaker Nancy Pelosi and other Congressional leaders. *(Source: Wikipedia)* **That's a FACT.**

Madge Moore showing the Daedalian Fighter Flight (Nellis AFB, NV) the WASP Congressional Gold Medal she was presented in Washington, D.C.

Regardless of their many accomplishments since their deactivation, the most important WASP legacy is their contribution as military pilots during World War II. Because of the expertise they demonstrated in successfully flying every type of military aircraft, from the fastest fighters to the heaviest bombers, the WASPs blazed a trail for women of future generations to follow. The WASP program had proven conclusively that female pilots, when given the same training as male pilots, were just as capable as men. *(Source: Wikipedia)* **That's a FACT.**

WASP Uniforms:

1. **<u>Trainee Field Dress</u>**: "general's" pants, white shirt   and overseas cap — no insignia

2. *Flying suit* with blue poplin cap — they usually did not fit!

3. <u>Dress Uniform</u>—**Santiago Blue** in color and including the **dress beret.**

WASPs were the only women in WWII to have berets.

The WASP Purse was one of the first "over the shoulder" bags.

4. <u>Winter flying suit</u> just like the men's suits.

5. <u>Battle jacket and slacks</u> (worn by most WASPs as a duty uniform). Normally worn with the blue poplin cap and not the beret shown in the picture.

*The Fifinella emblem (lower right in the image) was drawn for the WASPs by Walt Disney.

*During the fall of 1918, Walt Disney attempted
to enlist for military service. He was rejected
because he was under age — he was only
sixteen years old at the time. Instead, Walt
joined the Red Cross and was sent overseas
to France, where he spent a year driving
an ambulance and chauffeuring Red Cross
officials. His ambulance was covered from stem
to stern, not with stock camouflage, but with
cartoons.*

Walt Disney's Contribution to the War Effort

Lovable characters such as Thumper, Ferdinand the Bull, Dumbo, and Dopey were all featured as unit mascots over the course of World War II. Even Jiminy Cricket, Pinocchio's conscience, represented a chaplain's unit. Walt Disney also provided the emblem associated with the WASPs — Fifinella.

Fifinella was described as a winged, belligerent-looking female gremlin. Disney originally created the design for a proposed film based on Roald Dahl's book, *The Gremlins*. The story of Fifinella began in 1942 when Dahl, an ex-RAF-pilot, wrote *The Gremlins*, a fairy tale about the hazards of combat flying. In this incarnation, the word "fifinella" only refers to female gremlins as opposed to any specific one. Dahl took the name from the great "flying" filly, Fifinella, who won the Epsom Derby and Epsom Oaks in 1916, the year he was born.

When the WASPs asked to use it as their official emblem he granted them the rights. The original design had the small winged figure coming in for a landing with a red circle in the

The WASP logo conceived and created by Walt Disney Studios.

background; she is portrayed with horns, a yellow flight cap, a red top, yellow slacks, long black gloves, red high-top boots, and goggles. The WASPs, however, rather than having the figure in a landing pose, added a large bomb astride which the figure sat. They dressed her in a red coat and purple trousers and added a dark blue circle for extra impact. Still, there were many custom patches made, so form and color varied from patch to patch.

Fifinella put in appearances on WASP flight jackets and in many variations on the noses of bombers. One B-17G Flying Fortress, Fifinella (Serial #42-107030) of the 91st Bomb Group, was named after her. Fifinella was lost on August 13, 1944 on a bombing raid at Le Manoir, France. During the Korean War there was also a B-29 Superfortress (Serial #42-6569) of the 19th Bomb Group.

Disney provided mascots for many unites fighting in World War II. Some of them were existing Disney characters like Donald Duck (featured in more than 20% of all insignia created), but most times the Disney artists would provide drawings for mascots the units already had.

Disney's influence even pervaded Nazi prison camps providing a source of comfort to thousands. In 1943, Army Air Force Second Lieutenant Emmet E. Cook, Sr., a B-17 bombardier drew Donald Duck behind bars with the caption "I Wanted Wings." The emblem quickly became the unofficial mascot for the prison. His renditions of the military insignia provided amusement and a reminder of home for fellow POWs. *(Source Wikipedia.)*

Ben and Helen, 1944.

WASP PROLOGUE

As a 2nd Lieutenant, Ben R. Games, US Army Air Forces, was stationed at Goodfellow Army Air Field in San Angelo, Texas. He taught Army instructor pilots the Instrument Flight Rules and procedures (IFR). He and his wife, Helen, were expecting their first child in October 1944. He had just graduated from the US Army Instrument Instructors School at Texas A&M, Bryan, Texas, and was now instructing instruments in a North American AT-6 while awaiting his next assignment and the birth of Ben Jr. (Bud).

The buildup of the Army Air Forces for the invasion of Europe was a top priority for the Army at this point in history, and once or twice a week basic flight instructors were drafted for secret assignments. Ben had asked to be assigned missions near San Angelo, Texas, so that he could be present for the birth of his son. His current mission was to teach Army Liaison Pilots how to land on unprepared fields without lights at night.

The classes lasted for two nights, then another group of students would arrive. There were four students per class. He was assigned 10 new PT-17s to use for the classes. He had picked them up from the factory in Gainesville, Texas.

In the beginning, there were 10 instructors assigned to help with the training. At the end of the first night of flying, only four planes were left operational. To keep the program going, Ben became the instructor pilot and the other pilots taught the classroom work.

The flying was really a simple procedure, since the Liaison Pilots were actually going to be flying L2, L3, and L4-type aircraft. Ben had them set a speed of 50 mph and use the throttle to set a decent rate of 300 ft per minute. When the plane hit the ground, it would bounce and then the pilot would cut the throttle to idle and control the plane by the rudder with the stick full back.

To start the flight pattern, Ben would have a GI (enlisted soldier) walk out into a Texas cow pasture with a flashlight. When the man heard the sound of the engine, he would flash the light and hold it in the direction of the plane. This simple procedure worked well — at the end of the program there were still four operational planes.

Ben had no assigned students, and would pick a basic flight instructor pilot at random and teach him the IFR procedures in a AT-6 after he'd flown the assigned flying cadets each day. After they were certified, the pilots would receive secret orders for England a few days later.

One day, Ben was certifying a pilot when the commander of the flight standardization board came to the operations building. He announced that another draft had come in for a secret mission. He said that the pilot selected would have to leave for a secret base the next day.

Drafts like this had been announced often during the past two weeks. Word had come back from the pilots who'd been selected that the mission was to go to glider pilot school, infantry training, and then to England. No one knew what the missions were before the draft — they found out only when briefed by the Base Commander.

To be fair, the Flight Commander said, this draft would be conducted by putting everyone's name into his helmet. The name he drew would be the man to take the mission. As luck would have it, the commander drew Ben's name.

As Ben emptied his locker, one of the other pilots volunteered to go in Ben's place. He knew Ben wanted to be there for the birth of his baby. He also told Ben that all of the names in the hat had been his. Some of the other pilots also volunteered to take Ben's place, but he refused and left to pick up his orders.

The assignment was a top secret one sending him to Avenger Field in Sweetwater, Texas. His mission was to become a check pilot for the WASP (Women Airforce Service Pilots) program.

The WASPs and Nancy Harkness Love (third from left) received attention from newspapers and Hollywood in 1942. Loretta Young (second from left) is escorted away from a B-17. The other two escorts are unidentified

WASPs of WW II

Ben R. Games, PhD 1944

Remember General of the Army Air Forces Hap Arnold, and the head of the WASP program for the Army Air Forces, Jacqueline Cochran? During August 1944, I received secret 90-day TDY (Temporary Duty) orders to become an Army Check Pilot for the women pilots' program. My assignment was to Avenger Field, Sweetwater, Texas — the home of the WASP pilot flight training school. The US Army check pilot's job was to approve the women pilots before they could fly for the US Army Air Forces.

Avenger Field had no runways or flight control tower. It consisted of a 3000-foot by 3000-foot grass field that was laughingly called an airport. There was a tetrahedron as large as a small aircraft in the center of the field to indicate the direction of landing.

Jacqueline Cochran, head of the WASP program.

The field's wooden operations building was painted white and housed the Army check pilots' office as well as the office of the woman in charge of flight training. The offices were across the hall from each other and each had a large window that opened out onto the flying field.

The difference between the two offices was that the Army Check pilots' office was just one room with two desks and chairs for the Army pilots, while the WASP's operations office was two rooms. The WASPs had an outer office with room for a secretary and a small waiting room, plus an office where the woman in charge spoke to her girls in private.

TETRAHEDRON

(A device to show the direction of take-off & landings).

The device may be made of any
material. It is not necessary for
it to be moved by the wind.

A wind sock may be mounted
to help judge the wind speed.

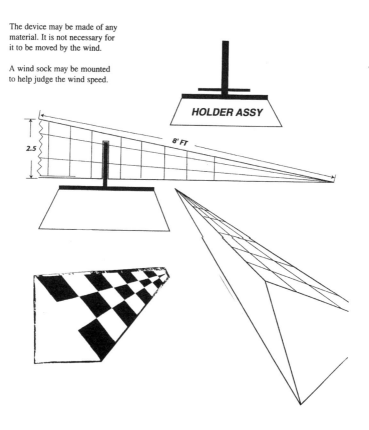

HOLDER ASSY

8' FT

2.5

There was no air-conditioning, but the window in each office opened to let in air from the outside. The doors of the offices opened into the hall. After a check ride, the women would enter the WASP outer office to wait while the Army check pilots went into their office to write out a grade slip and the result of the check ride.

It was a court marshal offence for an Army Instrument Check Pilot to speak to a WASP, this was especially enforced during or after a flight check. We were instructed not to even say "good morning," and to start immediately giving the women pilots direct instrument or flight instructions, such as "climb to three thousand feet and level off. Descend one thousand feet and turn left forty-five degrees."

We used the BT-13 for the instrument check ride. The woman pilot sat in the aft seat under a hood that completely covered the rear cockpit. There was an intercom between the two cockpits, as well as a 400 KC radio, but no radio compass. The check ride consisted of demonstrating basic control of the aircraft using flight instruments. There was no navigation or use of the Adcock Radio Range required to graduate.

The flying program required that the women fly their final instrument check ride, and then wait until the Check Pilot had delivered the grade slip to the WASP Operations Officer. The Operations Officer was in charge of the girl's flight training, and would then call each woman into her office to inform her whether she had passed or received a "pink slip." A pink slip was a failed flight check. If a woman received three pink slips, she was sent home.

This was basically the same system used for men in the cadet primary flight training program, except if a man washed out (failed) he was usually sent to navigation or bombardier school. Both flight schools used flying instructors who were civilian pilots. The instructor wore pilot wings with a large "S" on the shield. Only the Flight Check Pilots were military officers.

Two other significant differences between the requirements for men and women were that the men did not get washed out for failing an instrument check ride, and there were no restrictions on talking to the male pilots.

I almost forgot! There were also three special requirements for Check Pilots assigned to Avenger Field: 1. The assignment was temporary duty (TDY); 2. They had to be instrument rated and; 3. They had to be married.

***

On Avenger Field there were five Army check pilots commanded by a Captain. The first flight check of this day was an instrument flight check ride. It was the student's final check ride before graduation and assignment to Foster Field, Texas. If she graduated, she'd be towing targets for the fighter gunnery students flying P-40 fighters. She was the envy of all the other students, since there would be lots of flying on this assignment as well as a chance to fly Army fighters.

It was a slow day, with only one check ride scheduled, so our Captain assigned himself to this flight. Now, this particular student pilot was good. In fact, she was the best pilot our Captain had ever flown with.

After the flight was over, he told all of us what a good pilot she was. After hearing this, one of the other check pilots asked if he could fly with her. It was against regulations to speak to a student, and a male pilot could not ask a student to do anything. To allow the man to fly with this amazing pilot, the Captain gave her a pink slip. This meant the student would be scheduled for another check ride. His plan worked, and the next day she had to fly another check ride.

Remember ... if a girl failed three check rides, she was sent home.

This was the pilot's second instrument check ride. After this flight was over, the Lieutenant raved about how well she flew and how smoothly she flew instruments. I spoke up and said that there wasn't anybody that I couldn't screw up and I wanted to fly with her to prove it. *(Even as a second Lieutenant, I was confident.)*

There was a problem with that, though, since the only way I could fly with the student was to convince our Captain to approve another pink slip for her. To convince him, I had to come up with a way to make sure she wasn't sent home.

The plan was simple. I would write out a passing grade slip before we took off, and the check pilots would all sign it. The plan was approved.

Before the scheduled flight, the Army pilots gathered around the Captain's desk to help fill out the grade slip. We were laughing and joking about what to write in the remarks section.

What we didn't know was that all the women pilots, including the student in question, believed we were writing out a pink slip before I'd even started the aircraft's engine. They couldn't hear what was being said, but could see us through the window. It was apparent from our actions that we were enjoying writing the grade slip.

We gave her a perfect score — the highest grade slip anyone had ever received, of course she didn't know that. Because she suspected I was going to fail her, she was darned mad. I'd just created the greatest danger I have ever faced, and didn't even realize it!

There wasn't a cloud in the sky, and it had started to get hot when I walked out to the BT-13 carrying my parachute over my shoulder. The student pilot was older than most of the students I'd flown with — probably about 26

Army Check Pilot 2nd Lt. Ben R. Games.

years old — was looking at this flight as her last chance to be a part of the WASPs. She had a look on her face that should've warned me trouble was ahead, but I was a 20-year-old 2nd Lieutenant whose only thought was how I was going to screw up her flight check and what great fun it would be to give her the signed perfect score.

The student was already at the plane and had her parachute in the back seat when I got there. (Remember the rules about what you could say to a student?) All I could do was grin from ear to ear as I told her to get aboard and put the cover over the rear cockpit before I started the engine.

She didn't answer. She just glared at me, and I still didn't sense that my life was in danger.

After getting into the front cockpit, I started the engine and asked her if she could hear me over the plane's intercom. She said she could, so I taxied out and turned the plane toward the take off heading. I then told her she was going to make the takeoff while under the hood on instruments.

This wasn't in the rule book, but she didn't say anything. She took the control stick and shook it so I knew she had control. She advanced the throttle and made a perfect takeoff without a change in heading.

I instructed her to make a climbing turn of 90° to the right and then another 45° climbing turn to the left. The students were taught to make the first turn to the left and then the second to the right. I changed all the directions, and it didn't confuse her. She was good, but I had faith in my ability to make her screw up.

Next I put pressure on the left rudder pedal while she was in a turn. I held the pressure while she went through all the flight patterns in the check ride list. Next I had her bring the aircraft to a stall straight ahead. Just as the plane shuddered indicating it was about to stall, I released the pressure on the rudder, opened my canopy, and started hitting the outside of the fuselage with my hand while screaming.

All hell broke loose. She pushed forward on the stick until the plane was headed straight down. At the same time, she released the hood over the back cockpit and started calling me names. She was very unladylike.

All of this took place directly over Avenger Field, and she announced in an extremely loud voice (I believe they could hear her on the ground) that she was going to kill me. I was a strong lad, and I got the nose of the plane up, but now she was pulling back on the control stick.

That aircraft went through more positions than most pilots have ever flown. Suddenly I was able to fly with the wings level, but I couldn't see her in the aft cockpit. My immediate plan was to get the plane on the ground as soon as possible.

For those pilots who have never flown a BT-13, let it be known that the rear cockpit control sick has a spring-loaded pin that can be pulled out so the control stick can be removed. While I was flying toward the base leg for landing, the control stick came through the crash bar just missing the back of my head. That woman knew the BT-13 and had removed the control stick to try spearing me with it!

My defense was simply to stay below the rim of the cockpit where she couldn't reach me. The only problem was that I couldn't see the ground from this position. I solved this problem by doing snap rolls when I wanted to verify my position. As long as she couldn't find a way to prevent me from looking up, I had it made ... sort of.

There were no runways at this airport, just a big, open dirt field with a wind sock mounted on a tetrahedron in the center of the field. All I had to do was get on the ground without hitting anything. So, I made two snap rolls on the final approach to line it up for the center of the field.

**View of the front cockpit instruments,
note the control stick.**

I controlled the plane's airspeed until it hit the ground and bounced. When the plane bounced, I shut off the magneto switches. All of this was done while I kept my head below the rim of the cockpit, and continued dodging the control stick that she was using like a spear.

By this time, she had lost her cool completely. She opened the rear canopy, stood up in the rear cockpit, and started climbing while holding onto the crash bar. She was trying to get to where she could reach me with her club. I did the only thing a good pilot would do at that time in that place — I pushed forward on the rudder pedal and pushed on the right brake to cause the plane to ground loop. It did, and she was thrown over the left side as I dived out of the right.

Believe it or not, the plane finally came to a stop in front of the operations building. The woman pilot hadn't lost her control stick club, and was now running around the nose of the plane looking for me! Thankfully, I was fast enough that I could keep the plane between us.

I kept calling for the Army pilots to catch her so I could get away. They were a bunch of cowards though, and had locked themselves in the office. They were all watching through the window. After five trips around the plane, the other students came out and caught my attacker, and I ran to the building. One of the other check pilots let me into the check pilots' office.

The Captain took the grade slip we had all signed before the flight and turned it in to the WASP Operation Officer. Flying was canceled for the rest of that day and a special meeting was

WASP Mary Boles Nelson, Jacqueline Cochran, Ethel Sheehy, Dede Deaton, Lt. Col. Roy P. Ward (Commanding Officer of Avenger Field)

called in the gym for everyone except the Army check pilots.

All of the Army check pilots were restricted from the base except for Lieutenant Crew and myself. We were quartered in one of the student rooms with a vacant room on each side.

What I didn't know was that Lt. Crew had put a note on the bulletin board offering private instructions on how to pass a flight check ride. He had put it under a notice for policing the area. It

**WASPs enjoy dinner with Commanding General of
the Army, Hap Arnold.**

wasn't dated or signed and he thought it wouldn't
be found until our tour of duty was finished.

The next day, no check rides were scheduled.
In fact, flying was canceled for the next two
days. No one would speak to us and a note was
placed on the bulletin board saying that all Army
check pilots were to be in the gym at 2000 hours
the following day to meet with General Hap
Arnold.

We thought it was a joke. Then I received a
sealed letter that said that I was to meet with Mrs.

Cochran at 1900 the following day. Sure enough, I got to meet Mrs. Cochran *and* the Commanding General of the Army, Hap Arnold. They came to Sweetwater, Texas, just to meet me!

General Arnold introduced me to Mrs. Cochran, and she had some choice things to say to me. Her language was *not* nice.

My new assignment was flying P-40s, and the Army got one mean lady pilot.

Conclusion

This is a nonfiction short story about one flying episode involving the Women Army Service Pilots of WWII. It's about one woman who was on the cutting edge of a man's domain and what happened when she misunderstood a prank. It is also about how rules and regulations can be made for a good reason and still may cause a tragedy if they are misused.

This incident took place in October 1944, when Germany's defeat was known and the Allies had control of the skies over the Far East. It is also about a young Army pilot who had read how important women were in the defense of their country when Mussolini invaded Ethiopia.

The Mobilization Order issued by Haile Selassie to the Ethiopians in 1935 reads:

> "Everyone will be mobilized, and all boys old enough to carry a spear will be sent to Addis Ababa. Married men will take their wives to carry food and to cook. Those without wives will take any woman without a husband. Women with small babies need not come. The blind and those who cannot walk, or for any reason cannot carry a spear, are exempt. Anyone found at home after the receipt of his order will be hanged."

The author could not find this in the US Army rule book, but it's an easy order to understand. The peak strength of the US Military in WWII was 12.2 million troops. Of these, 350,000 were women volunteers. The US had 671,000 wounded in action, 292,000 killed, 59,000 aircraft lost, 157 military vessels lost, 866 merchant ships lost. The youngest US Serviceman was 12 years old. He was wounded in combat and given a Dishonorable Discharge for lying about his age.

God Bless the American Soldier
& God Bless America!

1. PERIOD COVERED	2. SHEET NO.
1975 Jul - Dec 1976 Jan - Jul	115

3. LAST NAME - FIRST NAME - MIDDLE INITIAL	4. SSN	5. GRADE, BRANCH, COMPONENT	ACTIVE DUTY
GAMES, BEN R.	▇▇▇▇	CW3 AVN	☒ YES ☐ NO

6. UNIT ASSIGNED OR ATTACHED FOR FLIGHT AND STATION	7. DMOS	8. SIGNATURE, TYPED NAME AND GRADE OF OPERATIONS OFFICER
Army Aviation Support Facility Grand Ledge, MI 48837	100BO	D. EDWARD CULLIMORE, CW3

SECTION I - SUMMARY OF PILOT EXPERIENCE

DUTY a	FIXED WING		ROTARY WING		OTHER f	TOTAL g	WX INST h
	SINGLE ENGINE b	MULTI ENGINE c	SINGLE ENGINE d	MULTI ENGINE e			
9. INSTRUCTOR PILOT	535	447	125	34	40	1181	
10. PILOT	1176	807	1282	717	689	4671	275
11. COPILOT	6	343	105	39	5	498	31
12. CIVILIAN PILOT	3914	2840	242		21	7017	
13. TOTAL TIME	5631	4437	1754	790	755	13367	306
14. COMBAT TIME				737		737	
15. FLT SIMULATOR / SYNTHETIC TRAINER					200		
16. OTHER							

SECTION II - FLIGHT HOURS ACCRUED - TOTAL HOURS FLOWN BY MONTH

JUL	AUG	SEP	OCT	NOV	DEC	JAN	FEB	MAR	APR	MAY	JUN
9	7	10	7	0	0	0	2	0	0	0	0

17. REMARKS

Jul
 0

DOB: 5 May 24

Aviation Schools:	Location	Aircraft Qualifications

Aviation Schools:
APFS Primary Flt Trng
Instructor Sch.(Pilot)
Instrument Instr Sch
P40 Flt Trng Sch
Air Craft Commander Sch
Aircraft Commander Scn
Radar & Elect Maint Sch
Auto Pilot Maint Sch.
Jet F 80 Pilot Tng
Jet F 86 Pilot Trng
Jet F 86D Pilot Trng
Jet Eng Maint Sch.
Radar Inter Off Sch
Disastor Oper Off Sch
Nuclear Safety Sch.
Air University USAF
Basic Helicopter Sch
UH 1 Helicopter Sch
Hel-Instrument Inst Sch
CH 47 Helicopter Sch
CH 34 Helicopter Sch.
Air Safety & Base Oper Sch.

Location
US Army
Randolph Fld,Texas
Bryan, Texas
Foster Fld,Texas
Ft Worth, Texas (B24
Roswell, N. Mex.(B29
Los Angles, Calif.
Grand Rapids, MI
Williams AFB, Arz
Nellis AFB , Nav.
Tyndall AFB, FL
Cincinnati, Ohio
Tyndall AFB. FL
Denver, Col.
Maxwell Fld, Ala
Maxwell Fld, Ala
USAAVAS
Ft Rucker , Ala.
USAAVAS
Ft Rucker, Ala.
Ft Rucker, Ala
USAAVAS

Aircraft Qualifications
Mil Aircraft

	Mil Aircraft
L2	UH 1, A,B,C,H
L3	OH 13G
L4	OH23 B, C
O1A	UH 19
U6A	CH 34
C47, DC3	OH 58
C54, DC6	CH 47 A,B, C
C46	Hughes 300
B25	OH6
AT7, D18	Brantly B2B
AT 11, C45	
F82,	
P61	All civilian air-
P80	craft listed in
P51	private pilot Log.
B24	
B29	
F94	
F86, F86D	
F84	

DA FORM 759
I MAY 74

PREVIOUS EDITION IS OBSOLETE.

Airpower Classics

Artwork by Zaur Eylanbekov

B-25 Mitchell

On April 18, 1942, Army Air Forces Lt. Col. James H. "Jimmy" Doolittle, leading a force of 16 B-25B medium bombers and crews, took off from the aircraft carrier USS *Hornet* and bombed Tokyo and other targets. It was the first time US aircraft had struck at Japan, and the raid immortalized both Doolittle and the B-25 Mitchell. The North American Aviation bomber went on to become a workhorse in every theater of World War II.

North American proposed the new Model NA-62, derived from a series of earlier prototypes, in a 1939 competition. The Army bought it right off the drawing board, ordering 184 of the airplanes. The clean, lean lines of the B-25 delivered good performance and facilitated both mass production and maintenance. Built in 10 major models, with numerous variants, the B-25 was particularly adaptable to field modifications. These included installation of heavy armament such as Paul I.

"Pappy" Gunn's fabled 75 mm cannon. The Mitchell was never the fastest, most maneuverable, or best-looking medium bomber. However, it grew to be the most heavily armed and was more versatile than any—even the German Junkers Ju 88.

Noted for its excellent handling characteristics, the B-25 performed remarkably well in many roles, including medium- and low-altitude bomber, close air support, photo reconnaissance, anti-submarine warfare, patrol, and—when occasion demanded—tactical fighter. Later it was used as a pilot and navigator trainer, and became much beloved in that role. In peacetime, it served as an executive transport, firefighter, camera airplane, test vehicle, and crop duster. The last B-25 trainers remained in service at Reese AFB, Tex., until finally retiring in January 1959—nearly 17 years after the bomber's most famous mission.
—*Walter J. Boyne*

This aircraft: USAAF B-25B Mitchell—*#40-2242*—as it looked in early 1942. It flew in the famous April 1942 Doolittle Raid over Tokyo, landed in Russia, and was scrapped there.

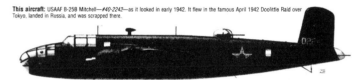

In Brief

Designed, built by North American Aviation ★ first flight Aug. 19, 1940 ★ crew of five or six (pilot, copilot, plus three or four of bombardier, radio operator, nav, bombardier, gunners) ★ two Wright R-2600 engines ★ number built 9,816 ★ **Specific to B-25J:** max speed 275 mph ★ cruise speed 230 mph ★ max range 1,275 miles (loaded) ★ armament (attack version) 16 .50 cal machine guns in nose, side, waist, top turret, tail turret ★ bomb load, up to 4,000 lb ★ weight (max) 41,800 lb ★ span 67 ft 7 in ★ length 53 ft 6 in ★ height 16 ft 4 in.

Famous Fliers

Medal of Honor: Ralph Cheli, James Doolittle, Raymond Wilkins. **Other notables:** 79 Doolittle Raiders (other than James Doolittle), H. H. Arnold, William Benn, Dwight Eisenhower, Thomas Gerrity, Paul Gunn, John Henebry, Joe Jackson (MOH in Vietnam), George Kenney, Robert Ruegg.

Interesting Facts

Named after airpower pioneer Billy Mitchell ★ built in numbers exceeding any other US medium bomber ★ used in World War II by Navy and Marine Corps as well as Australia, Britain, Canada, China, France, Holland, Soviet Union ★ pioneered thermal de-icing ★ crashed into cloud-shrouded Empire State building on July 28, 1945 ★ featured in films such as "Thirty Seconds Over Tokyo" (1944), "Catch-22" (1970), "Hanover Street" (1979), "Forever Young" (1992).

The B-25 became a true workhorse.

Amsie Games Doing What She Always Wanted To

By BILL SHEFFER

The Dutchess, a dowager beagle living with utter disregard for calorie counting, yawned and eyed the early morning activity at Sleepy Hollow Motor Motel, 1800 Cassopolis Street, Elkhart. Having seen more aircraft than most hounds have rabbits, she sensed someone in the family was going flying.

The Piper Pawnee B, a low-winged crop duster with a high camel back, waited a pilot with its long needle-nose pointed skyward and its white fabric jeweled in dew. It looked like a man's plane standing there along the chain fence at Elkhart North Side Airport.

Major and Mrs. Ben R. Games, an unconventional couple just reaching the age where life reportedly begins, left the living quarters of their modern motel, fastened safety seat belts and pointed their blue Thunderbird toward the airport a few minutes away.

Ben Games Jr., 20, his leg encased in a cast as the result of a skiing miscalculation in Michigan, remained behind to mind the motel as 11-year-old brother Jon, impatiently counting the years until he flies gliders, got

Mrs. Ben Games

ready for school. Young Ben is already a flier.

Ferry Pilot

Mrs. Games, the former Helen Marie Amsden of Goshen, has been a ferry pilot for the past six years and has logged more than 1,000 hours in the air since her solo flight at Midway Airport 15 years ago. The Pawnee "duster" was a new plane to her.

"Amsie," as her GHS classmates called her in '43, was flying cross-country from Lock Haven, Pa., to Oklahoma City, Okla., a distance of 1,247 air miles. Her job was to deliver the brand new $15,000 "duster" intact . . . alone in the single seater without radio control.

Eleven days after son Ben got his fixed-wing license on February 9, Helen had her helicopter rating and became the 86th woman to wear one of the silver Whirly-Girl medals. She's also a member of the Ninety-Nines, an international organization of women pilots which once numbered Amelia Earhart Putnam as its president.

Helen and her husband, a jet fighter pilot, have flown single and multi-engine aircraft over the country from plant to customer as the family hobby while developing their motel, mobile home court and Red Carpet Lounge over the past decade.

58

AUTHORS PERSONAL INFORMATION

Ben R. Games, PhD, Major, CW-4, TCNA-6, flew bombers and night fighters during WWII. Then Jet Fighters for the USAF during the Korean War, and Chinook helicopters in Vietnam for the 1st Cavalry Division. He is a member of the North American Mach Busters Club and of the Distinguished Flying Cross Society with 737 recorded combat hours.  After 35 years he retired from military flying in 1978 and later became the manager of the Turks & Caicos National Airline.

He served in Vietnam as a pilot with the 228 Aviation Battalion, Company B, 1st Cavalry Division, and is a life member of Army Aviation Class 43K, 1st Cavalry Division Association,

MOAA, USAF Association, VHPA, DFC Society, National Guard Association of the US, Camp Grayling Officers Club, VFW, American Legion, and the DAV.

During his military service Ben was awarded the Distinguished Flying Cross for Heroism, Bronze Star, 14 Air Medals, Army Commendation Medal with "V" Device, National Defense Service Medal w/3 Bronze Service Stars, MI Medals of Valor w/Oak leaf cluster, two Legion of Merit. Vietnam Campaign Medal w/1960 device, Republic of Vietnam Gallantry Cross w/Palm Unit Citation, and Republic of Vietnam Civil Actions Medal of Honor with First Class Unit Citation.

During the past fifty years stories of his flying adventures have been read by people around the world. They range from a child's Christmas story, biographical adventures, to science fiction.

To find out more about other books written by the author, visit:

www.FideliPublishing.com

Artist unknown, U.S. Coast Guard
Established in 1942, the U.S. Coast Guard Women's Reserve allowed women to partici-
pate in the war effort more directly. The service's acronym was derived from the Coast
Guard motto: Semper Paratus, Always Ready.

THE GUARDIAN ANGEL

Ben R. Games, PhD

A young boy watched the birds fly and thought, "Why can't I?"

Then in Sunday School he learned that Angels fly and thought, "Why can't I?"

The young man and woman holding hands stood looking up at the clouds in the sky and the woman said, "Why don't we fly?"

Now the Lord has a plan for all his children. He looked down and saw that they were getting ahead of the plan. If something wasn't done there would be a traffic jam at the Pearly Gates. He called the Archangel Michael and told him to think of ways to help the plan.

The Archangel formed a committee of Angels and told them that the Head Man had said to do something. They decided that every pilot must have a Guardian Angel to watch over him or her to see that they did not show up at the Pearly Gates before their time.

Then the Archangel went back to the Lord. He told him about the Committee and their idea. Then he asked the Lord which Angel to assign to the task. The Lord sighed and looked again. There were so many trying to fly that one Angel would never do. The Lord said, "These are my Children so assign all the Angels who watch over the children to take turns watching over pilots."

So it came to pass that every pilot was assigned a Guardian Angel to help see that he didn't get into heaven before his time.

Wasp Timeline — 1943

February 21 — Avenger Field in Sweetwater, Texas, welcomes its first class of women pilots.

February — The WFTD school in Houston, Texas closes.

March 21 — Cornelia Fort becomes the first woman to die on active duty for the United States when another pilot accidentally clips the wing of the plane she is flying.

August 5 — The Women's Auxiliary Ferrying Squadron (WAFS) merge with Jackie Cochran's training program to form the Women Airforce Service Pilots (WASP).

September 30 — Representative John Costello of California introduces the WASP militarization bill.

December 17 — The WASP wings are made available in time for the graduation of Class 43-W-8.

Mess hall, Avenger Field

Wasp Timeline — 1944

February — The WASPs are issued with Santiago Blue uniforms.

March 24 — Senators Joseph Hill (Alabama) and Harold Burton (Ohio) submit a resolution calling for the appointment of female pilots and aviation cadets into the Army Air Forces.

June — The congressional bid for WASP militarization fails.

July — Rumors begin circulating in the press that the WASP program is about to be disbanded.

October 1 — General Hap Arnold issues a memorandum to WASP Director Jackie Cochran stating the WASPs would "soon become pilot material in excess of needs."

October — The WASPs receive notification from that their unit would be disbanded in December.

November 1 — Brigadier General Bob Nowland writes a memo describing the hardships that will be caused by deactivating the WASP program.

December 7 — General Hap Arnold addresses the final graduating class of WASPs.

December 20 — The WASP program is deactivated.

DATE DUE

CPSIA information can be obtained at www.ICGtesting.com
Printed in the USA
LVIW01n0208260315
431936LV00001B/7

* 9 7 8 1 6 0 4 1 4 1 6 2 7 *